Alchemy

how medieval science paved
the way

Table of Contents

Intro

Medieval alchemy was a fascinating discipline that emerged during the Middle Ages and persisted until the early modern period. It encompassed a range of practices and beliefs that sought to transform and manipulate matter, particularly in the pursuit of turning base metals into noble metals like gold and silver. However, alchemy was not solely concerned with metallurgy; it also encompassed elements of philosophy, medicine, and spiritual pursuits.

During the medieval period, alchemy was deeply rooted in both Greek and Arabic traditions. Greek philosophers such as Aristotle and the Hellenistic alchemist Zosimos of Panopolis influenced early alchemical theories, while Islamic scholars made significant contributions to the field through their translations and commentaries on ancient Greek texts.

Alchemy was seen as a secretive and mystical practice, and alchemists often used symbolic language and allegories to convey their knowledge. They believed in the concept of transmutation, which involved the transformation of substances from one form to another. This idea was not limited to metals; alchemists sought to transmute the self and achieve spiritual enlightenment as well.

One of the primary goals of alchemy was the creation of the Philosopher's Stone, a legendary substance that was believed to possess transformative powers. It was thought to have the ability to transmute base metals into noble metals and grant eternal life. The quest for the Philosopher's Stone was a central focus of many alchemists during the medieval period.

Alchemy also had significant overlaps with early chemistry and medicine. Alchemists developed laboratory techniques, experimental methods, and apparatus that laid the groundwork for modern chemistry. They experimented with various substances, attempting to purify them and create new compounds. These experiments eventually led to advancements in the understanding of chemical processes.

Over time, the practice of alchemy gradually evolved into modern chemistry, as scientific methods and approaches gained prominence. The emergence of the scientific method in the 17th century, coupled with the work of figures like Robert Boyle, Antoine Lavoisier, and others, marked a shift away from the mystical and spiritual aspects of alchemy towards a more empirical and evidence-based approach.

While alchemy did not achieve its primary goal of turning base metals into gold or discovering the Philosopher's Stone, its legacy can still be seen in the development of chemistry and the understanding of natural processes. It also played a significant role in shaping the philosophical and cultural landscape of the Middle Ages.

Time boundaries

Medieval alchemy spanned a significant period of time, roughly from the 5th century to the 16th century. It emerged during the early Middle Ages and continued through the Renaissance, overlapping with the transition from the medieval period to the early modern era. Hermes Trismegistus is believed to have already written between the 1st and 3rd centuries A.D., during the Roman Empire, way ahead of medieval ages.

The specific time boundaries for medieval alchemy can vary, as historical periods are not always precisely defined. However, it is generally considered to have gained momentum during the 12th and 13th centuries and reached its peak of popularity in the 14th and 15th centuries.

During the early medieval period, alchemical knowledge was primarily derived from the translations and interpretations of ancient Greek texts, such as those attributed to Hermes Trismegistus. Islamic scholars in the Middle East played a crucial role in preserving and transmitting this knowledge, translating works from Greek into Arabic and making significant contributions of their own.

As the medieval period progressed, alchemy became more prominent in Western Europe. Many alchemical texts were translated from Arabic into

Latin, making them more accessible to European scholars. European alchemists began developing their own theories, practices, and experimental methods.

In the 14th and 15th centuries, alchemy experienced a surge of popularity in Europe. The spread of alchemical knowledge was facilitated by the development of the printing press, allowing for the wider dissemination of texts and ideas. Prominent alchemists during this period included figures like Ramon Llull, Geber, and Albertus Magnus.

As the Renaissance unfolded, alchemy started to undergo significant changes. The rise of humanism and the increasing emphasis on empirical observation and experimentation led to a more critical approach to alchemical practices. This transition marked the gradual shift from medieval alchemy to the development of modern chemistry, which began to distance itself from the mystical and spiritual aspects of its predecessor.

While medieval alchemy doesn't have a precise start or end date, it was most active and influential from the 12th to the 15th centuries, with its legacy carrying on into the early modern period.

Legality and Perception of Alchemy

The legality and perception of alchemy did undergo changes over the course of the medieval period. The practice of alchemy was subject to varying degrees of acceptance and scrutiny, often influenced by social, religious, and political factors.

In the early medieval period, alchemy was generally tolerated and even supported by certain rulers and institutions. Monarchs and nobles were often intrigued by the potential wealth that alchemical transmutation could bring, as the ability to turn base metals into gold was seen as a path to financial prosperity. Alchemists were sometimes employed by royal courts or wealthy patrons, who provided them with resources and protection.

However, as time went on, the perception of alchemy began to shift. The Church, which held significant influence during the Middle Ages, became increasingly suspicious of alchemy due to its association with occult practices and its potential for fraud. Alchemical pursuits that were perceived as attempts to create gold or eternal life were viewed as sinful and deceptive.

In the 14th and 15th centuries, there was a growing backlash against alchemy. Laws were enacted in some regions to control and restrict its practice. For example, in England, King Henry IV issued a decree in 1404 that prohibited the transmutation of metals and the use of alchemical practices for personal gain.

Despite these legal restrictions and the Church's condemnation, alchemy continued to be practiced in various forms throughout the medieval period. Many alchemists operated discreetly, sharing their knowledge within secretive circles and using cryptic symbolism to protect their teachings from scrutiny. Alchemical texts often contained allegorical language and complex codes, making them difficult for outsiders to understand.

It's worth noting that alchemy was a diverse field, and not all alchemists were solely focused on transmutation or the Philosopher's Stone. Some alchemists explored medicinal applications, herbal remedies, and chemical processes that laid the foundation for advancements in pharmacy and chemistry.

Overall, the legality and societal acceptance of alchemy fluctuated throughout the medieval period. It faced both support and opposition from various quarters, with its reputation evolving as cultural, religious, and political contexts shifted.

Prominent Alchemists

Hermes Trismegistus

Hermes Trismegistus, often referred to as Hermes the Thrice-Greatest, is a legendary figure in the realm of alchemy, esotericism, and ancient wisdom. Hermes Trismegistus is believed to be a combination of the Greek god Hermes (known as Mercury in Roman mythology) and the Egyptian god Thoth.

Hermes Trismegistus is associated with a body of writings known as the Hermetica or the Corpus Hermeticum. These texts, believed to have been written between the 1st and 3rd centuries A.D., encompass a wide range of topics including philosophy, theology, astrology, magic, and alchemy. They were highly influential in the development of Western esoteric traditions.

The Hermetic texts attributed to Hermes Trismegistus emphasize the interconnectedness of the spiritual and natural realms. They convey the idea that there is a divine wisdom or hidden knowledge that can be accessed through contemplation, spiritual purification, and the study of natural phenomena. This wisdom is often referred to as "Hermetic knowledge" or "Hermeticism."

In alchemy, Hermes Trismegistus is regarded as one of the founding figures, with his teachings forming the basis of alchemical philosophy. The alchemical concept of the unity of opposites, as well as the idea of transmutation and spiritual transformation, can be traced back to the Hermetic tradition associated with Hermes Trismegistus.

The figure of Hermes Trismegistus has had a profound impact on Western esoteric and philosophical traditions. The Renaissance period witnessed a revival of interest in Hermeticism, with figures like Marsilio Ficino and Giordano Bruno incorporating Hermetic ideas into their works. The Hermetic texts continue to be studied by scholars interested in the history of ideas, spirituality, and the occult.

It's important to note that the attribution of the Hermetic texts to an actual historical figure named Hermes Trismegistus is a matter of debate among scholars. The texts themselves may be a compilation of writings from different authors over time, but they are commonly associated with the legendary Hermes Trismegistus.

His influence on alchemy, philosophy, and esoteric traditions cannot be denied. The ideas and teachings attributed to Hermes Trismegistus have shaped the understanding of spiritual and mystical pursuits for centuries.

Geber (Jabir ibn Hayyan)

Geber, also known as Jabir ibn Hayyan, was a prominent alchemist, chemist, and philosopher who lived during the 8th and 9th centuries in the Islamic Golden Age. He is considered one of the most influential figures in the history of alchemy and is often referred to as the father of Arabic alchemy.

Geber authored numerous works on alchemy, totaling over a thousand treatises. These writings covered various aspects of alchemical theory, laboratory practices, chemical reactions, and the preparation of medicinal substances. Geber's works were instrumental in advancing alchemical knowledge and shaping the development of the field.

Geber emphasized the importance of experimentation and observation in alchemy. He believed that practical laboratory work was crucial for understanding the nature of matter and the processes of transmutation. Geber developed precise experimental techniques, such as distillation and crystallization, which became foundational practices in alchemical laboratories.

Geber introduced a systematic classification of substances based on their properties. He categorized materials into three main groups: spirits (volatile substances), metals, and compounds. This classification system served as a foundation for later alchemical and chemical classifications.

Concept of Sulfur and Mercury: Geber introduced the concept of sulfur and mercury as essential components of matter. These substances were seen as representing the active and passive principles, respectively, and played a significant role in alchemical transformations. Geber's understanding of sulfur and mercury influenced subsequent alchemical theories and symbolism.

Equipment and Apparatus: Geber developed and improved various laboratory equipment and apparatus used in alchemical experiments. He invented new types of distillation apparatus, including the alembic, which enabled the separation and purification of substances. Geber's advancements in apparatus and techniques contributed to the practical aspects of alchemy.

Geber's works had a profound impact on alchemical practices in the Islamic world and beyond. His ideas were widely studied and expanded upon by later alchemists, both in the Islamic tradition and in Europe during the Middle Ages. Geber's works were translated into Latin and became influential in medieval Europe, shaping the development of Western alchemy.

Geber's contributions to alchemy extended beyond practical laboratory techniques. He explored philosophical and metaphysical aspects of alchemy, delving into the symbolism and spiritual dimensions of the discipline. His works integrated alchemy with Islamic philosophy, mysticism, and religious thought, emphasizing the pursuit of both practical knowledge and spiritual enlightenment.

Albertus Magnus

Albertus Magnus, also known as Saint Albert the Great, was a medieval alchemist, philosopher, theologian, and natural scientist. He lived from around 1193 to 1280 and made significant contributions to various fields of knowledge during his lifetime.

Education and Academic Career: Albertus Magnus was born in Germany and joined the Dominican Order at a young age. He studied at the University of Padua and later became a prominent lecturer at universities in Germany and France, including the University of Paris. He taught and wrote on a wide range of subjects, including theology, philosophy, logic, and the natural sciences.

Albertus Magnus sought to harmonize philosophy and theology, viewing them as complementary disciplines. He drew heavily from the works of ancient philosophers such as Aristotle and incorporated their ideas into Christian theology. His integration of Aristotelian philosophy into Christian thought was influential in medieval scholasticism.

Alchemy and Natural Science: Albertus Magnus had a deep interest in natural science, including alchemy. He conducted experiments and investigations in the field, contributing to the understanding of various chemical processes. He explored topics such as the properties of minerals, the preparation of medicines, and the transmutation of metals.

Aristotelian Influence: Albertus Magnus was one of the key figures responsible for reintroducing the works of Aristotle to Western Europe. He studied and commented extensively on Aristotle's writings, helping to shape the way Aristotle's philosophy was understood and incorporated into Christian thought.

Influence on Thomas Aquinas: One of Albertus Magnus's most significant contributions was his influence on the philosopher and theologian Thomas Aquinas. Albertus was Aquinas's teacher, and he played a vital role in shaping Aquinas's philosophical and theological ideas. Aquinas referred to Albertus as "my master" and incorporated many of his teachings into his own works.

Albertus Magnus was recognized for his holiness and wisdom, and he was canonized as a saint in 1931 by Pope Pius XI. He is considered the patron saint of scientists and philosophers.

Albertus Magnus's extensive writings, which covered topics ranging from theology to natural science and alchemy, had a lasting impact on intellectual thought in the Middle Ages. His emphasis on observation, experimentation, and the integration of philosophy and theology laid the foundation for the development of later scientific pursuits and influenced the course of Western intellectual history.

Ramon Llull

Ramon Llull, also known as Raymond Lull or Raimundus Lullus, was a philosopher, theologian, mystic, and alchemist who lived during the 13th century. He was born in 1232 or 1233 in the Kingdom of Majorca, which is present-day Spain. Llull is notable for his extensive writings and his innovative approach to knowledge and communication.

Ars Magna: Ramon Llull is best known for his system of thought called the Ars Magna ("The Great Art"). The Ars Magna was an intricate system of logic and combinatorial mathematics aimed at generating knowledge and revealing universal truths. Llull's system utilized symbols and combinations to represent concepts, which could then be used to generate new knowledge.

Llull believed that a universal language, understood by all, was necessary for effective communication and the dissemination of knowledge. He proposed a method of combining basic elements of language to create a universal system of communication. This idea influenced subsequent thinkers, including Leibniz's concept of a universal symbolic language.

Llull's philosophical and theological works touched upon various subjects, including metaphysics, ethics, and the nature of God. He sought to reconcile philosophical ideas with Christian theology, emphasizing the rational exploration of truth while maintaining a strong religious foundation.

Mystic and Contemplative: Llull was deeply influenced by his spiritual and mystical experiences. He engaged in intense periods of contemplation and prayer, seeking a direct connection with the divine. Llull's mystical experiences played a significant role in shaping his philosophical and theological perspectives.

Llull had an interest in alchemy and the medicinal properties of substances. He believed that alchemical processes and the preparation of remedies could contribute to physical healing and spiritual transformation.

Ramon Llull's ideas and writings had a lasting impact on various fields, including philosophy, theology, linguistics, and logic. His innovative approach to knowledge generation and his emphasis on universal communication influenced later thinkers, and his ideas continued to be studied and debated long after his death.

His work demonstrated a unique blend of rational inquiry, mystical contemplation, and an interdisciplinary approach to knowledge. His contributions to philosophy, theology, and the development of a universal language laid the groundwork for subsequent intellectual and linguistic endeavors. Today, Llull is recognized as an important figure in the history of Western thought and continues to be studied for his innovative ideas and methods.

Paracelsus

Paracelsus, born as Philippus Aureolus Theophrastus Bombastus von Hohenheim, was a significant figure in the field of alchemy, medicine, and natural philosophy during the 16th century. He was born in 1493 or 1494 in Switzerland and is known for his revolutionary ideas and contributions to medical science.

Rejection of Traditional Medicine: Paracelsus criticized the prevailing medical practices of his time, particularly the reliance on ancient authorities such as Galen and Avicenna. He believed in the importance of observation, experience, and the individuality of patients, advocating for a more empirical and personalized approach to medicine.

Paracelsus developed his own system of medicine, which came to be known as "Paracelsian Medicine" or "iatrochemistry." He emphasized the use of chemical remedies, the understanding of diseases as imbalances in the body, and the importance of treating the whole person rather than just the symptoms.

Three Principles and the Doctrine of Signatures: Paracelsus proposed a tripartite view of the human body, identifying three principles—sulfur, mercury, and salt—that corresponded to the spiritual, mental, and physical aspects. He also promoted the concept of "Doctrine of Signatures," which suggested that the outward appearance of plants could indicate their medicinal properties.

Chemical Philosophy: Paracelsus believed that metals and minerals had medicinal properties and could be used for therapeutic purposes. He explored the extraction of active ingredients from various substances and experimented with different chemical processes. His investigations laid the groundwork for the development of pharmaceutical chemistry.

Paracelsus contributed to the understanding of the effects of substances on the human body. He recognized that the dose and concentration of a substance were critical factors in determining its toxicity, laying the foundation for the field of toxicology.

Influence on Renaissance Thought: Paracelsus's ideas challenged the established medical and philosophical doctrines of his time. His rejection of authority and his emphasis on personal experience and experimentation influenced the broader Renaissance spirit of inquiry and the development of modern scientific thought.

Paracelsus's unconventional and iconoclastic approach to medicine and alchemy earned him both admiration and criticism during his lifetime. His ideas sparked debates and controversy, but his emphasis on observation, experimentation, and the holistic understanding of the human body contributed to the advancement of medical science.

Heinrich Cornelius Agrippa

Heinrich Cornelius Agrippa von Nettesheim, commonly known as Heinrich Cornelius Agrippa, was a 16th-century German occultist, writer, theologian, and philosopher. He lived from 1486 to 1535, and his works had a significant impact on the fields of magic, occult philosophy, and hermeticism. Agrippa's writings explored a wide range of subjects, including occultism, natural philosophy, astrology, and the mystical traditions of his time.

"Three Books of Occult Philosophy": Agrippa's most famous work is "De Occulta Philosophia Libri Tres" or "Three Books of Occult Philosophy." Published in 1531, this comprehensive treatise examined various aspects of occultism, including natural magic, ceremonial magic, divination, and the influence of celestial bodies. The work drew from a wide range of sources, including Jewish, Christian, and hermetic traditions.

Agrippa sought to synthesize the teachings and beliefs of different philosophical and mystical traditions, blending elements from Greek, Jewish, and Christian thought with hermetic and magical practices. He aimed to explore the unity and interconnectedness of various branches of knowledge.

Agrippa was influenced by the philosophy of Neoplatonism, which emphasized the existence of a transcendent unity and the mystical ascent of the soul towards the divine. This influence is evident in his mystical and philosophical writings, where he explored the nature of the soul, the hierarchy of beings, and the divine presence in the universe.

Reputation and Controversy: Agrippa's works were both praised and criticized during his time. He faced opposition from religious authorities due to his exploration of occult subjects, and his writings were sometimes seen as heretical or dangerous. Agrippa himself was accused of practicing magic, but he maintained that his interests were purely intellectual and philosophical.

Agrippa's works had a significant impact on the development of Western esoteric traditions. His ideas and writings influenced subsequent occultists, magicians, and philosophers, including figures like John Dee and Aleister Crowley. The "Three Books of Occult Philosophy" became an important reference for occult practitioners and scholars throughout the centuries.

Other Works: In addition to the "Three Books of Occult Philosophy," Agrippa wrote on various topics, including natural philosophy, theology, and the defense of women against accusations of witchcraft. Some of his other notable works include "De Vanitate" (On the Vanity of Arts and Sciences) and "De Nobilitate et Praecellentia

Foeminei Sexus" (On the Nobility and Excellence of the Feminine Sex).

Heinrich Cornelius Agrippa's writings played a significant role in the dissemination of occult knowledge and the development of Western esoteric traditions. Although his ideas and works were met with controversy during his time, they continue to be studied and appreciated by scholars, occultists, and those interested in the history of esoteric thought.

Alchemists' Achievements and Legacy

Coded Language

Alchemists developed a coded language as a means of concealing their knowledge and practices from the uninitiated. This coded language served multiple purposes, including preserving secrecy, protecting intellectual property, and avoiding persecution from religious or political authorities.

The coded language used in alchemy can be attributed to several factors:

Secrecy and Protection: Alchemists guarded their knowledge closely, considering it valuable and powerful. By employing a coded language, they aimed to keep their methods and discoveries within a select circle of practitioners. This secrecy also protected alchemists from potential accusations of heresy or witchcraft, as their writings appeared cryptic to outsiders.

Metaphoric and Symbolic Language: Alchemists heavily relied on symbolism, allegory, and metaphors in their writings. They used coded terms and elaborate analogies to represent substances, processes, and concepts. This allowed them to communicate their ideas in a way that required interpretation and understanding by those familiar with alchemical symbolism.

Hiding Practical Details: Alchemical texts often concealed precise instructions for laboratory procedures or recipes. Instead, they presented abstract philosophical concepts, mystical teachings, and symbolic descriptions. This intentional obscurity made it difficult for non-alchemists to decipher the practical aspects of alchemy without proper guidance or initiation.

Religious and Philosophical Justifications: Alchemists sometimes justified their coded language by invoking religious or philosophical doctrines. They presented their writings as esoteric teachings, suggesting that deeper spiritual truths were hidden within the encoded text. This approach elevated alchemy to a higher, more spiritual level and contributed to the aura of mystery surrounding the field.

It's important to note that the development of the coded language in alchemy varied across time periods, regions, and individual alchemists. Different symbols, terms, and metaphors were used by different practitioners, leading to variations in alchemical writings. Some common elements in alchemical symbolism include the use of animals, metals, planets, and mythical figures to represent different aspects of the alchemical process.

The coded language of alchemy also had a significant influence on the development of Western esoteric traditions and occultism. It inspired subsequent generations of occultists and mystics who continued to explore hidden knowledge and symbolic systems.

Today, scholars of alchemy analyze and decipher the coded language used by alchemists, unraveling the hidden meanings and practical instructions embedded within the texts. By studying alchemical symbolism and the historical context in which these writings were produced, researchers can gain insights into the practices and philosophies of alchemists.

Overall, the coded language of alchemy is an integral part of its rich legacy, contributing to the intrigue, mysticism, and enduring fascination surrounding this ancient discipline.

Metaphorical Language

The esoteric nature of alchemical knowledge required a specialized language that could convey complex ideas, spiritual concepts, and practical instructions in a concise yet veiled manner. The use of symbols and metaphors allowed alchemists to communicate profound philosophical and spiritual insights without explicitly revealing their secrets.

Personal and Spiritual Transformation: The use of colorful language and symbolic imagery in alchemy was also intended to facilitate personal and spiritual transformation. By engaging with cryptic texts and decoding their hidden meanings, alchemists believed that aspiring adepts could undergo an inner journey of self-discovery and illumination, gradually unraveling the mysteries of the universe.

Amplifying Concepts: Alchemical symbolism and metaphorical language were employed to amplify concepts and ideas beyond their literal meanings. By using vivid imagery and poetic expressions, alchemists sought to evoke emotional and intellectual responses, stimulating deeper contemplation and understanding of the profound principles underlying their work.

Unifying Different Disciplines: Alchemical language was influenced by various cultural, philosophical, and mystical traditions. Alchemists integrated concepts from philosophy, astrology, mythology, and religious teachings into their writings. This interweaving of diverse sources created a rich tapestry of symbolism that transcended individual disciplines, forming a unique alchemical language.

The colorful language of alchemy adds to its mystical allure and enduring fascination. It serves as a gateway into the alchemical mindset and worldview, allowing us to explore the symbolic and metaphorical dimensions of their philosophical and practical pursuits. Although decoding and understanding alchemical texts can be challenging, their language and symbolism continue to inspire and captivate those interested in the history, philosophy, and symbolism of alchemy.

The Philosopher's Stone

The Philosopher's Stone is a legendary substance that holds great significance in alchemical traditions. It is a central concept in alchemy and was believed to possess powerful transformative properties. The pursuit of the Philosopher's Stone was a primary goal for many alchemists during the medieval and early modern periods.

The exact nature and properties of the Philosopher's Stone varied in different alchemical texts and traditions, but there were some common elements.

One of the primary functions attributed to the Philosopher's Stone was its ability to transmute base metals, such as lead or copper, into noble metals like gold or silver. This process was seen as a metaphorical and literal transformation, representing the purification and perfection of matter.

The Philosopher's Stone was also believed to possess profound healing properties. It was considered a universal panacea capable of curing diseases, rejuvenating the body, and prolonging life. The Stone was thought to hold the key to achieving physical and spiritual immortality.

The quest for the Philosopher's Stone was not solely about material gains. Alchemists believed that its discovery would also lead to spiritual enlightenment and the attainment of higher consciousness. It was seen as a means to attain wisdom, enlightenment, and a deeper understanding of the natural world.

The descriptions of the Philosopher's Stone in alchemical texts often utilized symbolic language and allegories. The Stone was associated with various symbols, such as the sun, the moon, and the phoenix, representing the transformative powers and cycles of nature.

It's important to note that the concept of the Philosopher's Stone was not purely literal but carried metaphorical and philosophical meanings. Alchemical texts often employed coded language and obscure symbolism to safeguard the knowledge from the uninitiated and to convey deeper philosophical teachings.

While the Philosopher's Stone remained elusive, the pursuit of this legendary substance played a significant role in the development of alchemical practices. It stimulated experimentation, the search for hidden knowledge, and advancements in laboratory techniques, contributing to the evolution of chemistry as a scientific discipline.

In the broader context of history, the idea of the Philosopher's Stone has captured the imagination of many, appearing in myths, legends, and literary works beyond the realm of alchemy. Its symbolism continues to resonate, representing the human quest for transformation, enlightenment, and the search for the ultimate truth.

The Philosopher's Tree

The concept of the "philosopher's tree" is a metaphorical representation in alchemy that symbolizes the process of transformation and the pursuit of spiritual and philosophical enlightenment.

The philosopher's tree is not a literal botanical tree but a symbolic representation of the alchemical process and its stages. It is often depicted as a diagram or a graphical representation, resembling a tree with branches, roots, and various symbols associated with alchemical elements, substances, or principles.

The philosopher's tree embodies the alchemical belief in the unity of opposites, such as the union of masculine and feminine principles, the reconciliation of heaven and earth, or the integration of the spiritual and material realms. The branches and roots of the tree symbolize the interconnectedness and harmony of these opposing forces.

The philosopher's tree illustrates the different stages of the alchemical process, which may include purification, separation, conjunction, fermentation, and coagulation. Each stage represents a step towards the refinement and transformation of the alchemist's own being, as well as the transmutation of base substances into spiritual gold or the philosopher's stone.

The symbols and elements associated with the philosopher's tree vary depending on the alchemical tradition or interpretation. They can include symbolic representations of planets, metals, elements, astrological signs, or spiritual concepts. These symbols convey the multifaceted nature of alchemical work and the integration of diverse elements into a unified whole.

The philosopher's tree encompasses both personal and universal transformation. It represents the alchemist's inner journey of self-discovery, spiritual realization, and the attainment of enlightenment. At the same time, it symbolizes the universal principles and cosmic processes that govern the transformation of all matter and existence.

The philosopher's tree serves as a visual representation of the alchemical path, encapsulating the alchemist's quest for spiritual and philosophical wisdom, the integration of opposing forces, and the transmutation of the self and matter. It is a powerful symbol that encapsulates the transformative nature of alchemy and its goal of achieving higher states of consciousness and understanding.

The Elixir of Life

The Elixir of Life is a legendary substance that is said to grant immortality or significantly prolong human life. It has been a subject of fascination and pursuit throughout various historical and mythical traditions, including alchemy.

The concept of an elixir or potion with life-extending properties can be traced back to ancient civilizations. In various cultures, including Egyptian, Chinese, and Indian, myths and legends revolve around the search for immortality or rejuvenation through a divine elixir or plant.

In the context of alchemy, the Elixir of Life was believed to be a product of alchemical transmutation, a substance that could confer longevity, restore health, and provide spiritual enlightenment. Alchemists sought to discover and create this elixir through their experiments and research.

The composition and preparation of the Elixir of Life varied across different alchemical traditions and texts. Alchemical recipes described the use of various ingredients, such as rare herbs, metals, minerals, or compounds. These ingredients were subjected to alchemical processes, including distillation, purification, and transmutation, to produce the elixir.

The quest for the Elixir of Life held symbolic significance within alchemy. It represented not only the pursuit of physical immortality but also the quest for spiritual enlightenment and the transformation of the human spirit. The process of creating the Elixir of Life mirrored the alchemist's own spiritual journey towards self-realization and transcendence.

Beyond its literal interpretation, the Elixir of Life also held allegorical meanings. It symbolized the union of opposites, the harmony of body, mind, and spirit, and the attainment of ultimate wisdom. The pursuit of the Elixir of Life was seen as an inner quest for inner transformation and self-mastery.

Historical Legacy: The concept of the Elixir of Life has had a significant impact on Western culture, inspiring literary works, myths, and legends throughout history. It continues to capture the imagination and fascination of individuals interested in the realms of mysticism, spirituality, and immortality.

Aurum Potabile

Aurum Potabile, which translates to "drinkable gold," is a term used in alchemy to refer to a medicinal elixir or tincture made from gold. It was believed that this preparation could possess curative properties and confer various health benefits.

The use of gold in medicinal preparations dates back to ancient times. In alchemy, gold was considered a noble metal associated with the sun and believed to possess unique qualities that could be extracted and harnessed for medicinal purposes.

The production of Aurum Potabile involved specific alchemical procedures. Alchemists aimed to extract the medicinal essence of gold by subjecting it to various treatments such as dissolution, purification, and separation techniques. These processes were intended to refine and concentrate the beneficial properties of gold.

The concept of the "Doctrine of Signatures," attributed to Paracelsus and other alchemists, played a role in the use of Aurum Potabile. According to this doctrine, substances in nature exhibited signs or resemblances that indicated their medicinal properties. Gold, with its radiant and incorruptible nature, was believed to symbolize its potential therapeutic effects.

Beyond its literal use, Aurum Potabile also held symbolic and allegorical significance in alchemical philosophy. It represented the pursuit of spiritual enlightenment and the transformation of the human spirit. The ingestion of Aurum Potabile was seen as a metaphorical consumption of divine wisdom and an elevation of consciousness.

Aurum Potabile was believed to have diverse health benefits. It was thought to strengthen the vital forces of the body, improve overall health and well-being, and counteract the effects of aging. The elixir was often used in traditional medicinal practices, particularly within the context of alchemy and alternative healing methods.

The use of Aurum Potabile diminished over time as alchemy transitioned into modern chemistry and the pursuit of more evidence-based medical practices. However, it remains an intriguing aspect of alchemical history and the exploration of alternative therapeutic approaches.

It is essential to note that the medicinal claims attributed to Aurum Potabile have not been scientifically validated or endorsed by modern medicine. The use of gold in medicinal preparations is not considered a mainstream medical practice today.

Aurum Potabile represents the alchemical fascination with extracting and harnessing the hidden properties of substances, in this case, gold, for therapeutic purposes. It reflects the alchemist's quest for both physical and spiritual well-being, seeking to unlock the transformative potential believed to reside within natural elements.

Alchemical Distillations

Alchemical distillations were a fundamental aspect of alchemical practices and laboratory techniques. Distillation was a method employed by alchemists to separate and purify substances by exploiting their different boiling points. Through this process, alchemists aimed to extract the essential or purified components of various substances for further experimentation and use.

The primary purpose of alchemical distillation was the separation of substances based on their volatility. By subjecting a mixture to heat, alchemists could vaporize the more volatile components, leaving behind the less volatile ones. This allowed for the extraction and isolation of specific substances of interest.

Alchemists utilized various types of distillation apparatus, including alembics, retorts, and stills. These vessels were designed to heat the mixture, collect the vapor, and condense it back into a liquid form for collection.

Basic Distillation Process: The process of alchemical distillation involved the following steps:
1. The mixture or substance to be distilled was placed in the distillation vessel.

2. The vessel was heated, typically using an external heat source such as a furnace or a bain-marie.
3. As the mixture was heated, the more volatile components vaporized and rose through the neck of the vessel.
4. The vapor was then directed into a condensing apparatus, such as a coil or a condenser, where it cooled and returned to a liquid state.
5. The condensed liquid, known as the distillate, was collected separately from the remaining non-volatile residue.

In some cases, alchemists performed multiple distillations or fractional distillations to further purify the substances. This involved collecting and re-distilling the condensate to separate different components based on their varying boiling points. Each distillation step aimed to refine and concentrate the desired substance.

Alchemical distillation held symbolic and metaphorical significance within the broader context of alchemy. It represented the purification and transformation of substances, mirroring the alchemist's spiritual journey toward self-realization and the attainment of higher knowledge.

Alchemical distillations were used for various purposes. They allowed alchemists to isolate and concentrate specific chemical compounds, extract essential oils from plants, purify metals, and create tinctures, elixirs, or other alchemical preparations.

Alchemical distillations played a crucial role in the alchemical laboratory, providing a means to separate, purify, and concentrate substances for further experimentation and practical applications. The distillation process, along with other alchemical techniques, contributed to the accumulation of chemical knowledge and the development of subsequent scientific disciplines such as chemistry and pharmacology.

Today, distillation remains a significant process in the fields of chemistry, industry, and essential oil extraction. While alchemical distillations were often embedded in symbolic and mystical contexts, they formed the basis for subsequent advancements in scientific distillation techniques.

The techniques and principles of alchemical distillations have undoubtedly influenced and laid the foundation for modern distillation processes in the chemical industry. While there are significant differences between the practices of alchemy and modern chemistry, some fundamental concepts and methods remain applicable.

Purpose and Objective: Both alchemical distillations and modern chemical distillations serve the purpose of separating and purifying substances. However, the objectives have shifted from mystical or philosophical pursuits in alchemy to practical and industrial applications in the modern chemical industry.

Equipment and Technology: Alchemical distillations were typically carried out using glassware apparatus, such as alembics and retorts, heated by furnaces or bain-maries. In contrast, the modern chemical industry employs sophisticated distillation equipment, such as column stills, fractionating towers, or distillation columns, which allow for continuous or large-scale operations. The use of modern technologies, automation, and control systems has significantly improved the efficiency, precision, and scalability of distillation processes.

Precision and Control: Modern distillation processes focus on precise control of temperature, pressure, and flow rates to optimize separation and achieve desired purity levels. In contrast, alchemical distillations often relied on empirical observations and qualitative assessments rather than precise measurements and control.

Alchemical distillations were performed within the context of alchemical theories, which incorporated mystical and symbolic elements. Modern chemical distillations, on the other hand, are grounded in scientific principles and a deeper understanding of chemical properties, thermodynamics, and phase equilibria.

Alchemical distillations were primarily used in the purification and isolation of substances for spiritual or medicinal purposes. In contrast, the modern chemical industry employs distillation techniques in a vast range of applications, including the separation and purification of chemicals, the production of fuels, the recovery of solvents, the production of pharmaceuticals, the purification of water, and more.

Alchemical distillations were often conducted on a small scale, in laboratory settings or individual workshops. In contrast, the modern chemical industry performs distillation processes on an industrial scale, employing large-scale distillation units capable of processing significant quantities of feedstock or raw materials.

Despite these differences, the principles and techniques developed through alchemical distillations paved the way for the advancement of modern chemical distillation practices. The understanding of boiling points, vapor-liquid equilibrium, phase separations, and the separation of complex mixtures are rooted in the foundations laid by alchemical experimentation and observations.

Today, distillation remains a vital process in the chemical industry, contributing to the production of a wide range of essential products and materials. The advancements in distillation technology and the integration of scientific principles have revolutionized the efficiency, scale, and precision of distillation processes, enabling significant advancements in chemical synthesis, purification, and separation techniques.

Spagyric Preparations

Spagyric preparations are a specific branch of alchemical practices that focus on the extraction and purification of medicinal essences from plants and minerals. The term "spagyric" derives from the Greek words "spao" (to separate) and "ageiro" (to bring together). It emphasizes the dual process of separation and recombination involved in these preparations.

Spagyric preparations aim to extract the essential components of plants and minerals while purifying them to their purest form. This process involves the separation of the plant or mineral into its different constituents (separation), followed by the recombination of these purified parts (recombination). The goal is to create a potent and purified substance that embodies the medicinal properties of the original material.

The first step in spagyric preparations is the separation of the plant or mineral into its different components. This process often involves maceration, fermentation, or distillation to extract the essential oils, volatile compounds, or other desired substances from the raw material. The remaining residue, known as the "caput mortuum," represents the impure or incombustible matter.

After the separation step, the extracted substances are purified through various alchemical processes, such as filtration, sublimation, or calcination. These processes eliminate impurities and unwanted elements, enhancing the purity and potency of the extracted substances.

In the final stage of spagyric preparations, the purified components are recombined. The essential oils or volatile compounds obtained during the separation step are reintroduced to the purified residue or "caput mortuum." This process aims to reestablish the unity and synergy of the plant or mineral, resulting in a final spagyric preparation.

Herbal Alchemy: Spagyric preparations often focus on medicinal plants and herbs. Alchemists believed that each plant possessed a unique signature and corresponding medicinal properties. By employing spagyric techniques, they sought to unlock and concentrate the healing essence of these plants.

Spagyric preparations were utilized for therapeutic purposes, including the creation of tinctures, elixirs, essences, or herbal remedies. These preparations were believed to possess enhanced medicinal properties compared to the original plant material, as the extraction and purification processes aimed to concentrate and refine the beneficial compounds.

Gold

Alchemists and their fascination with gold were closely intertwined. Gold held a prominent place in alchemical philosophy and practices for several reasons:

Gold was seen as the pinnacle of perfection, both physically and spiritually. Alchemists regarded gold as a symbol of divine and incorruptible matter. It represented the culmination of the alchemical transformation process, where base metals were believed to be transmuted into gold, mirroring the alchemist's own spiritual journey toward enlightenment and perfection.

One of the primary goals of alchemists was to discover the Philosopher's Stone, a legendary substance believed to have the power to transmute base metals into gold. This quest for transmutation was seen as both a literal and metaphorical pursuit, representing the transformation of the base self into a purified and elevated state.

Gold was also valued for its alleged medicinal properties. Alchemists believed that gold contained vital energies and healing properties that could be harnessed for medicinal purposes. Aurum Potabile, the drinkable gold, was one of the preparations created to extract the medicinal essence of gold. It was believed to possess curative properties and was used in alchemical and medical practices.

Alchemists conducted extensive studies and experiments with various metals, including gold. They sought to understand the nature of metals, their properties, and how they could be manipulated through alchemical processes. This exploration contributed to advancements in metallurgy and the understanding of metalworking techniques.

It is important to note that while alchemists sought to transmute base metals into gold, the literal transmutation of metals remains an elusive goal that has not been scientifically achieved. However, their pursuit of the transmutation of metals, including gold, played a significant role in the development of chemistry, metallurgy, and the scientific understanding of matter and its transformations.

The association of alchemists with gold and the quest for transmutation contributed to the enduring fascination and symbolism surrounding alchemy. Today, the alchemical symbolism of gold continues to captivate imaginations, inspiring philosophical, artistic, and spiritual exploration.

Black Magic?

Alchemists were often associated with accusations of practicing black magic or sorcery, particularly during periods of intense religious fervor and witch trials. However, it is important to distinguish between the actual practices of alchemy and the perception of alchemists as practitioners of black magic.

The secretive and esoteric nature of alchemical practices, along with their use of symbolic language and mystical concepts, contributed to the perception that alchemists were engaged in dark or occult arts. The public and religious authorities often had limited understanding of alchemical principles and interpreted the practices through their own beliefs, which sometimes led to misconceptions and accusations of black magic.

Supernatural Associations: Alchemists' pursuits of transmutation, the search for the Philosopher's Stone, and the use of symbolism and ritualistic elements contributed to the association with mystical and supernatural practices. The aura of mystery and the belief that alchemists possessed hidden knowledge and powers sometimes led to unfounded accusations of engaging in black magic or sorcery.

The historical periods when alchemical practices were prevalent, such as the Middle Ages and the

Renaissance, were marked by religious conflicts, superstitions, and widespread beliefs in witchcraft and occult practices. Alchemists often worked in parallel with individuals who were indeed involved in the occult or esoteric practices, contributing to the blurring of boundaries and associations.

The accusations of practicing black magic or sorcery were often rooted in religious and political motivations. Religious authorities sought to maintain orthodoxy and eliminate perceived heresies or practices that challenged their power. Alchemists, with their unconventional pursuits and claims, sometimes became targets of religious persecution.

Alchemists employed secrecy and encoded language in their writings to safeguard their knowledge and protect their intellectual property. This inclination for secrecy, combined with the limited understanding of their practices by outsiders, further fueled suspicions and perceptions of engaging in forbidden or black arts.

It is important to recognize that the association between alchemists and black magic was largely a product of the historical context and the perceptions of the time. Alchemists, for the most part, were focused on experimentation, the pursuit of knowledge, and practical applications such as medicine and metallurgy. While they operated within a mystical and philosophical framework, their objectives were distinct from the malevolent practices associated with black magic.

Modern understanding of alchemy acknowledges its historical significance as a precursor to scientific disciplines such as chemistry and acknowledges the distinction between alchemical pursuits and accusations of practicing black magic or sorcery.

Dragon Blood

The term "dragon's blood" has been associated with alchemy and herbal medicine, although it is important to note that it does not refer to the literal blood of dragons. Instead, "dragon's blood" refers to a resin obtained from various plant species, particularly those belonging to the genera Dracaena and Daemonorops.

"Dragon's blood" resin has a rich red color and was highly valued for its unique properties. Alchemists attributed symbolic significance to the resin, associating it with qualities such as power, protection, purification, and transformation.

In herbal medicine and folklore traditions, "dragon's blood" resin was believed to possess various medicinal properties. It was used topically for wound healing, as an astringent, and for treating skin conditions. It was also employed in ritualistic practices and as an ingredient in incense and potions associated with protection, banishing negative energies, and enhancing magical workings.

Alchemists incorporated "dragon's blood" into their practices and symbolism. It represented the fiery and transformative nature of alchemical processes, as well as the ability to transmute and purify base substances. The resin was sometimes included in alchemical recipes and preparations as a symbolic ingredient, emphasizing the alchemist's pursuit of transformation and spiritual enlightenment.

Alchemists developed various formulations and preparations that incorporated "dragon's blood" resin, such as tinctures, elixirs, or powders. These formulations were believed to possess specific properties and were utilized for both medicinal and symbolic purposes within the alchemical framework.

It is important to differentiate the symbolic and metaphorical use of "dragon's blood" in alchemical practices from its literal interpretation as the blood of mythical creatures. The association between "dragon's blood" and alchemy reflects the alchemist's utilization of natural substances, such as resins and plant extracts, within their philosophical and practical pursuits.

Today, "dragon's blood" resin continues to be used in various spiritual and occult practices, as well as in natural remedies and incense blends. However, it is crucial to approach these uses from a perspective of cultural symbolism and historical context rather than a literal belief in mythical creatures.

Black or Cold Dragon

The references to the "black dragon" or the "cold dragon" in the context of alchemy are metaphorical and symbolic rather than literal depictions of mythical creatures. These terms are used to represent specific alchemical concepts and processes.

Black Dragon: In alchemical symbolism, the black dragon often represents the prima materia or the initial substance from which the alchemical transformation begins. It is associated with chaos, darkness, and the hidden potential within matter. The black dragon represents the unrefined, impure, and chaotic state of the starting material, which is to be transformed and purified through the alchemical processes.

Cold Dragon: The cold dragon is another metaphorical representation in alchemical symbolism. It refers to the cooling or condensing aspect of the alchemical process, often associated with the principle of fixation. In the alchemical worldview, the cold dragon represents the solidifying and stabilizing force that transforms volatile or gaseous substances into a more fixed and stable state.

Both the black dragon and the cold dragon symbolize key stages of the alchemical transformation, where the alchemist works to transmute base materials into a purified and perfected form. The alchemical journey involves the processes of separation, purification, and recombination, leading to the attainment of the Philosopher's Stone or the desired goal of spiritual and material transformation.

The swallowed up Sun

The concept of the "swallowed up sun" is a metaphorical and symbolic expression found in alchemical texts. It represents an important alchemical process known as the sol niger or the black sun. Here's an explanation of its symbolism:

The sol niger, Latin for "black sun," is a stage in the alchemical process of transformation. It represents the stage of putrefaction or decomposition, where the alchemist works with the prima materia (the initial substance) to break it down and dissolve its impurities. The sol niger is often associated with darkness, chaos, and the descent into the underworld.

The metaphor of the "swallowed up sun" is used to describe the sol niger stage. It signifies the loss of light, the dissolution of the ego, and the descent into the shadowy depths of the alchemical work. The sun, a symbol of illumination, is metaphorically consumed or absorbed into darkness during this stage.

The sol niger and the concept of the "swallowed up sun" are symbolic of the inner transformative journey pursued by the alchemist. It represents the process of confronting and working through the shadow aspects of the self, the unconscious, and the reintegration of fragmented or hidden elements of the psyche.

The sol niger stage is not the end of the alchemical process but a necessary phase leading to integration and rebirth. Through the dissolution and putrefaction of the prima materia, the alchemist seeks to purify and recombine its essential components. This process paves the way for the emergence of the lapis philosophorum, the philosopher's stone, which represents the culmination of the alchemical work and the attainment of enlightenment or perfection.

The "swallowed up sun" is a vivid metaphorical expression that captures the symbolic depth and transformative nature of the sol niger stage in alchemy. It represents the alchemist's journey into the darkness, the dissolution of the self, and the subsequent integration and rebirth necessary for spiritual and material transformation.

Porcelain

Alchemists played a significant role in the development and refinement of porcelain, a ceramic material highly regarded for its beauty and durability.

The alchemical pursuit of transmutation and the quest for the philosopher's stone involved experimentation with various materials, including ceramics. Alchemists sought to understand the nature of matter and its transformation through processes such as calcination, fusion, and purification. Their explorations in ceramics contributed to advancements in the understanding of materials and the development of porcelain.

Porcelain is a type of ceramic material composed primarily of kaolin, a fine white clay, and other materials such as feldspar and quartz. Alchemists, particularly in China, were involved in the refinement of porcelain production techniques, including the selection of suitable clay, the development of glazes, and the firing processes. Their experiments and knowledge of materials and firing temperatures helped refine the quality and appearance of porcelain.

China has a rich history of porcelain production, and alchemical principles influenced its development. Chinese alchemists, through experimentation and refinement, developed tech-niques for producing high-quality porcelain with distinct characteristics. They discovered methods to achieve vitrification, where the clay particles fuse together to create a glass-like, translucent material. The Chinese alchemists' knowledge of kiln technology and material properties played a significant role in the advancement of porcelain production.

In Europe, alchemical knowledge brought from the East influenced the development of porcelain manufacturing. In the 16th and 17th centuries, European alchemists, particularly in Germany, were involved in efforts to reproduce Chinese porcelain. Their knowledge of materials, glazes, and firing techniques contributed to the establishment of porcelain production centers, such as Meissen in Germany and later, other European porcelain factories.

Alchemists' experiments and observations in porcelain production also contributed to scientific understanding. Their investigations into the behavior of materials during firing, the effects of different additives and glazes, and the development of kiln technology laid the foundation for advancements in ceramic science and the understanding of material properties.

The development of porcelain owes much to the alchemical insights and experimentation of the past. The alchemists' pursuit of transmutation and their exploration of materials and processes laid the groundwork for the refinement of porcelain production techniques, leading to its esteemed status as a valuable and beautiful ceramic material.

Hessian Crucibles

The term "Hessian crucibles" refers to crucibles made from Hessian clay, also known as Hessian sand or fire clay. Crucibles are vessels or containers used in high-temperature processes, such as melting or refining metals, in alchemy and other scientific disciplines.

Hessian clay is a type of fire clay that is highly refractory and can withstand high temperatures without cracking or deforming. It is known for its ability to withstand thermal shocks and chemical reactions with molten metals. Hessian clay gets its name from the region of Hesse in Germany, where it was originally sourced.

Alchemists utilized crucibles extensively in their experiments and operations involving metals. Crucibles were used for processes such as smelting, calcination, fusion, and the preparation of various alchemical preparations. Hessian crucibles, with their excellent refractory properties, were particularly suitable for withstanding the high temperatures required in these operations.

Hessian clay crucibles had several advantages in alchemical practices. They had a high resistance to thermal shock, meaning they could withstand rapid temperature changes without cracking. This property was crucial for processes involving the heating and cooling of materials. Hessian crucibles also exhibited good chemical resistance, making them suitable for handling a wide range of substances, including corrosive or reactive materials.

Hessian clay crucibles were typically handmade. The clay was shaped into crucible form and then fired at high temperatures to enhance its refractory properties and strength. The firing process transformed the clay into a hard, durable material capable of withstanding the extreme conditions encountered during alchemical operations.

As alchemy evolved into modern chemistry, the use of crucibles continued but with advancements in materials and technology. Various other materials, such as porcelain, graphite, and high-temperature ceramics, became common choices for crucible manufacturing. These materials offered even greater resistance to heat and chemical reactions, enabling more sophisticated experiments and processes.

Hessian crucibles made from Hessian clay played a significant role in alchemical practices, providing a reliable and durable container for high-temperature operations. They contributed to the advancement of alchemical techniques and the understanding of metallurgy, laying the foundation for subsequent developments in the field of chemistry and materials science.

Accountability

The level of accountability for alchemists, regardless of their specialty, varied depending on the specific time, place, and social context in which they practiced.

Alchemists often encountered scrutiny from religious authorities, particularly during periods when the Church held significant influence. The Catholic Church, for instance, considered certain alchemical practices as potentially heretical or in conflict with orthodox religious teachings. Alchemists could face accusations of engaging in forbidden arts, blasphemy, or sorcery, which could lead to investigations, trials, and punishments.

Alchemical practices were subject to legal regulations that varied across different regions and periods. Authorities might impose restrictions on the possession and use of certain substances, equipment, or processes related to alchemy. Unauthorized experimentation or the production of counterfeit materials could result in legal consequences and penalties.

Alchemists often sought the patronage and protection of influential individuals, such as royal or noble patrons, to mitigate potential accountability. Patronage provided a degree of legitimacy and support, shielding alchemists from legal or religious scrutiny. Powerful patrons could also intervene on their behalf and offer protection from accusations or persecution.

Alchemists' credibility and accountability were often tied to their reputation and the perceived effectiveness of their work. Positive results, such as successful transmutations, the production of valuable substances, or the development of useful medicines, enhanced their standing and protected them from scrutiny. Conversely, failure to deliver promised outcomes or being associated with fraud could damage their reputation and lead to accountability.

Alchemists often formed communities and networks of like-minded practitioners, sharing knowledge and experiences. Within these circles, there could be informal mechanisms of accountability, with peers evaluating and challenging each other's work. Reputation within the alchemical community played a role in holding practitioners accountable to their peers' expectations and standards.

In comparison, modern scientists generally operate within a framework that recognizes and protects intellectual property rights, emphasizes empirical evidence, and provides legal safeguards for their research activities. While scientists today are subject to legal and ethical frameworks, their work is not typically seen as heretical or inherently subversive, and they are less likely to face severe legal consequences for their pursuits.

It is important to acknowledge the significant historical and cultural differences between the world of alchemy and the contemporary scientific community. The legal challenges faced by alchemists reflect the social, religious, and intellectual climate of their time, which differed greatly from the legal landscape scientists navigate today.

Alchemists had literally skin in the game, modern day scientists don't.